THE NATURE KIDS GUIDE TO

SLOTHS

DAVID ANDERSON

LP Media Inc. Publishing
Text copyright © 2026 by LP Media Inc.

For information address LP Media Inc. Publishing,
30012 Variolite St NW, Princeton MN 55371
www.lpmedia.org

Publication Data

Sloths
The Nature Kid's Guide to Sloths — First edition.

Summary: "Learn all about Sloths, the Nature Kid Way"
— Provided by publisher.

ISBN: 979-8-89818-100-0

[1. Sloths – Non-Fiction] I. Title.

Title: The Nature Kid's Guide to Sloths

CONTENTS

TREETOP HOMES

Rustle! A sloth hangs from a tall tree branch. It moves very slowly.

Sloths live in **tropical rainforests**. These forests are warm and wet all year. This weather helps tall trees grow close together. Their branches form a thick **canopy** high above the ground.

Sloths spend most of their lives in trees. They eat, sleep, and rest up in the branches. Some sloths come down only once a week!

The rainforest canopy is the perfect home for sloths. Leaves grow everywhere, and vines connect the trees. Sloths can also climb down to the ground to move between trees.

JUNGLE LIFE

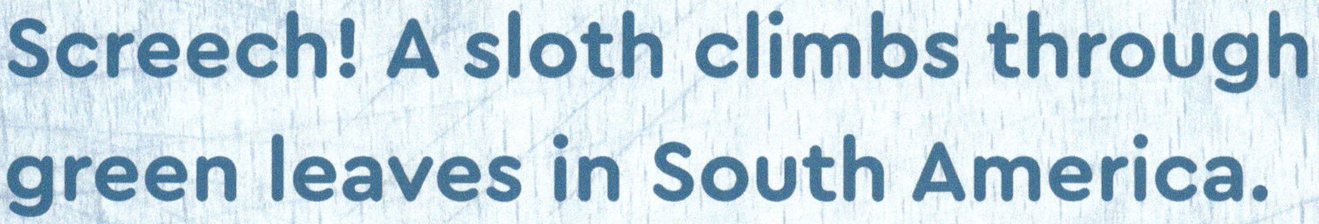

Screech! A sloth climbs through green leaves in South America.

Sloths live only in Central and South America. They are found in many countries. Brazil, Costa Rica, and Panama all have sloths.

Different sloths live in different areas. Two-toed sloths live from Nicaragua to Brazil.

Sloths need forests with many trees. They cannot live in dry or cold places. Rainforests give them all they need.

The pygmy three-toed sloth lives on just one tiny island off the coast of Panama.

SLOW
LIVING

Thump! A sloth drops to the forest floor. It is small and light.

Sloths are about the size of a medium dog. They weigh 8 to 20 pounds. This makes them light enough to live high in the trees.

Two-toed sloths are larger than three-toed sloths. They can grow up to 27 inches long. That is about as long as a baseball bat!

This small size helps sloths survive. Their light bodies let them hang from thin branches without breaking them.

A sloth's stomach can make up one third of its total body weight when full of food!

9

COOL CLAWS

DID YOU KNOW?
Sloth claws are so curved that sloths cannot walk well on flat ground at all!

Click! A sloth grips a branch with its long claws.

Sloths have long, curved claws. These claws can be 3 to 4 inches long. That is longer than your fingers!

Two-toed sloths have two claws on each front foot. Three-toed sloths have three claws on each front foot. All sloths have three claws on their back feet.

Sloth claws work like strong hooks. They wrap around branches and hold tight. Sloths can hang for long periods with very little effort. Their claws lock in place while they rest.

SNIFF IT

Sniff! A sloth lifts its nose in the misty morning air.

Sloths have a great sense of smell. They use their noses to find food in the trees. A sloth can sniff out its favorite leaves from far away.

Smell helps them know which leaves are safe to eat. Some leaves can make sloths sick or even poison them. Their noses help them tell the difference.

Sloths can also smell other sloths nearby. Mothers and babies use scent to find each other in the forest. This is helpful because their eyesight is not very good

Sloths sometimes grab their own arms thinking they are branches!

HIDE AND
SEEK

Shhh! A sloth stays very still in the trees. It blends right in.

Sloth fur is brown or gray. This color matches the tree bark where sloths live. Predators have a hard time seeing them.

Algae also grow on sloth fur. This makes sloths look green. The green color helps them hide even better in the leafy trees.

Sloths move very slowly. This helps algae grow on them. Their fur is the perfect home for the tiny plants.

Some sloths have so much algae that moths live in their fur and eat it!

LEAFY LUNCH

Chomp! A sloth chews a green leaf slowly. It is a tasty snack.

Sloths eat mostly leaves. They munch on leaves from many different trees. Cecropia tree leaves are a favorite food.

Sloths also eat some flowers and fruit. They find these treats high in the treetops.

Leaves do not give much energy. This is one reason sloths move so slowly. Their bodies work hard to digest tough leaves. It can take a month to digest one meal!

Sloths rarely drink. They get enough water from the juicy leaves they eat!

SLOTH SIGNALS

Rustle! A sloth hangs still in the Cecropia tree.

Sloths are very quiet animals. They do not roar or bark. They make soft sounds that are hard to hear. Baby sloths squeak when they want their mothers.

Sloths use their bodies to talk. A sloth may hiss if it feels scared. It opens its mouth wide. This shows its teeth as a warning.

Mother sloths and babies find each other by sound. The baby makes a high cry. The mother follows the sound through the trees. Sloths also use smell to send messages to other sloths nearby.

WATCH
OUT

Swoosh! An Eagle flies over the trees. A sloth freezes.

Sloths have many **predators**. Harpy eagles hunt sloths from the sky. These huge birds grab sloths with sharp **talons**. Jaguars climb trees to catch sloths too.

Ocelots and snakes also hunt sloths. These predators look for movement in the trees.

Sloths are most at risk on the ground. They must climb down to go to the bathroom about once a week. Predators can catch them more easily then.

Harpy eagle talons are as big as grizzly bear claws! They can grab an adult sloth and fly away!

22

Hiss! A snake slithers near. The sloth stays perfectly still.

Staying still is a sloth's best trick. When danger is near, sloths freeze in place. They do not run or fight. They just stop moving.

This works very well. Predators hunt by looking for movement. A frozen sloth looks like part of the tree.

Sloths can hold still for hours. Their slow heartbeat helps them stay calm.

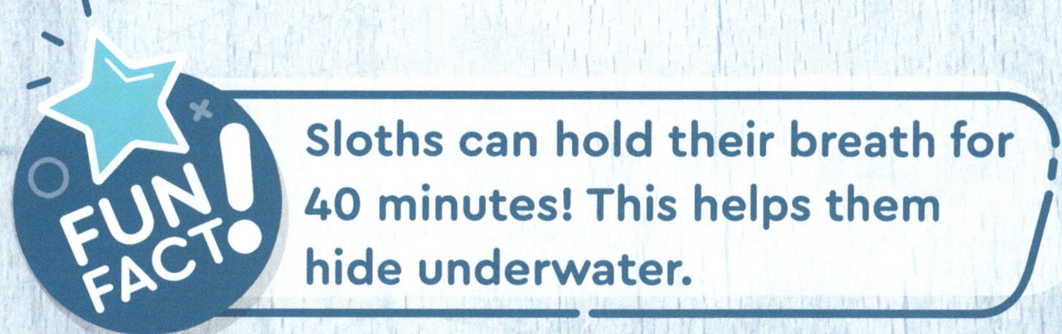

SLOW MOTION

Snap! A branch bends slowly under a sloth inching along.

Sloths rank among Earth's slowest mammals. They move only about six feet per minute in trees. On the ground, they are even slower barely crawling along at around 1 foot per minute.

Sloths move slowly to save energy. Their leaf diet does not give them much fuel.

Slow movement also keeps sloths safe. A creeping sloth is hard for predators to spot.

Sloths can swim three times faster than they move on land using their long arms.

SNOOZE TIME

Yawn! A sloth closes its eyes high in a tree. It is time for a long nap.

Sloths sleep a lot. They rest about ten hours each day in the wild. Some sloths in zoos sleep even longer.

Sloths sleep while hanging from branches. They curl into a ball, and their strong grip keeps them safe.

Sloths are most active at night. This is when they wake up to eat leaves in the dark. Then they go back to sleep.

Baby sloths learn to sleep by clinging to their mothers for the first few months of life!

SOLO
SLOTHS

A sloth hangs alone in a tall tree. It likes the quiet.

Sloths live alone most of the time. They do not stay in groups. Each sloth has its own space in the forest.

Sloths only meet up to mate. After that, they go back to living alone.

Mother sloths stay with their babies for about six months to a year. The baby clings to its mother's belly as she moves through the trees. When the young sloth grows up, it leaves to find its own part of the forest.

A sloth's home range can overlap with other sloths. They just ignore each other.

SCREAMING
SWEETHEARTS

Howl! A female sloth makes a loud cry from a high branch.

Female sloths make loud screaming sounds. These calls can be heard far away, echoing through the forest.

Male sloths hear these calls and climb toward the sound. This can take many hours because sloths move so slowly.

Sloths mate while hanging from branches. After mating, the male leaves, but the female stays in her home range.

A female sloth's scream can be heard up to 700 meters away through the dense rainforest!

CUTE CUBS

Chirp! A tiny two-toed baby sloth clings to its mother's belly.

Baby sloths are called pups. They are born with fur and open eyes. These tiny newborns weigh less than one pound.

Pups hold onto their mothers for months. They grip her fur tightly as she climbs through trees. This keeps them safe up high.

Young sloths drink their mother's milk at first. Later, they start to nibble leaves. Pups learn which plants to eat by watching their mothers.

Baby sloths are born with all their claws already fully formed and ready to grip tightly onto their mother's fur!

HOLD TIGHT

Grunt! A mother sloth wraps one arm around her pup.

Mother sloths carry their babies everywhere. Pups ride on mothers for up to seven months, clinging tightly to her chest and belly fur.

Baby sloths learn how to climb by copying their mothers. They also learn which trees are safe to visit.

After about one year, young sloths are ready to live alone. The mother then moves away to a new area. The young sloth keeps the mother's home range.

Mothers lick their babies' faces to teach them which leaves to eat!

36

Crash! A tree falls in the forest. A sloth loses its home.

Sloths need trees to survive. But people cut down trees for farms and roads. When trees fall, sloths lose their homes.

Sloths move very slowly on the ground. This makes it hard for them to survive without trees.

Some sloths cross roads to find new trees. But crossing roads is dangerous for them.

When forests are cut down, sloths sometimes travel on power lines to reach new trees. Their strong claws help them grip!

SAVING
SLOTHS

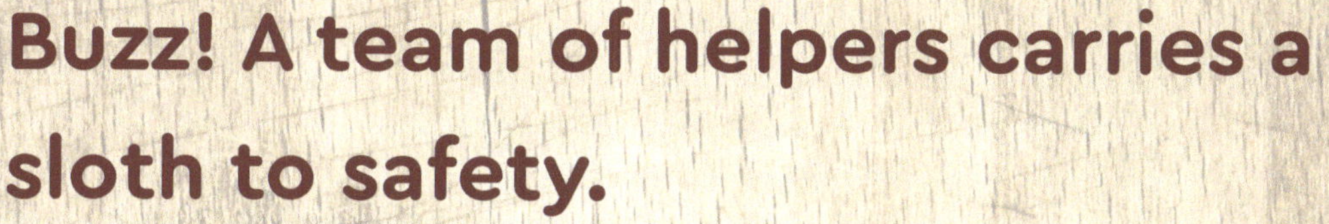

Buzz! A team of helpers carries a sloth to safety.

Many people work to help sloths. Rescue centers care for hurt and orphaned sloths. Workers feed them and help them get strong.

Some groups plant new trees for sloths. More trees mean more homes. Other groups build rope bridges to help sloths cross roads safely.

Kids can help too by learning about rainforests! You can also raise money for sloth rescue centers or adopt a sloth through a wildlife group.

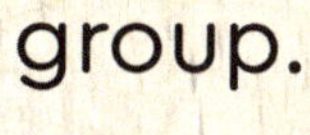

Rescue centers use special forest cages that let sloths come and go until ready!

GLOSSARY

canopy
The top layer of a forest where tree branches and leaves grow close together.

tropical rainforests
Warm, wet forests where it rains a lot and many plants and animals live.

algae
Tiny green plants that can grow on wet things like sloth fur.

predators
Animals that hunt and eat other animals for food.

talons
The sharp, curved claws that birds like eagles use to catch animals.